SO-BFA-066

To Rooster,
our favorite
movie maker!

Happy 9 years old!

Love,

Kirsten, Eric &
the chickens

Anya, maroon, Gretta,
& Miriam

(+ one black dog)

movie maker!

MAKING MOVIES

Writing, Producing, and Directing Movies

by Geoffrey M. Horn

GARETH**STEVENS**
GS
PUBLISHING
A Member of the WRC Media Family of Companies

Please visit our Web site at: www.garethstevens.com
For a free color catalog describing Gareth Stevens Publishing's
list of high-quality books and multimedia programs, call
1-800-542-2595 (USA) or 1-800-387-3178 (Canada).
Gareth Stevens Publishing's fax: (414) 332-3567.

Library of Congress Cataloging-in-Publication Data

Horn, Geoffrey M.
    Writing, producing, and directing movies / by Geoffrey M. Horn.
        p. cm. — (Making movies)
    Includes bibliographical references and index.
    ISBN-10: 0-8368-6841-2 — ISBN-13: 978-0-8368-6841-8 (lib. bdg.)
        1. Motion pictures—Juvenile literature. I. Title. II. Series: Horn,
    Geoffrey M. Making movies.
    PN1994.5.H67   2006
    791.43—dc22   2006004074

This edition first published in 2007 by
Gareth Stevens Publishing
A Member of the WRC Media Family of Companies
330 West Olive Street, Suite 100
Milwaukee, WI 53212 USA

This edition copyright © 2007 by Gareth Stevens, Inc.

Concept: Sophia Olton-Weber
Managing Editor: Valerie J. Weber
Art direction and design: Tammy West
Picture research: Diane Laska-Swanke

Photo credits: Cover, Warner Brothers/Photofest; p. 5 © Paramount/courtesy
Everett Collection; p. 6 Paramount Pictures/Photofest; p. 9 Newmarket Films/
Photofest; p. 12 Warner Independent Pictures/Photofest; pp. 14, 18 © Focus
Features/courtesy Everett Collection; pp. 17, 22 © Warner Brothers/courtesy
Everett Collection; p. 19 © New Line/courtesy Everett Collection; pp. 21, 29
Twentieth Century Fox/Photofest; p. 26 © Universal/courtesy Everett
Collection; p. 27 Universal Studios/Photofest

All rights reserved. No part of this book may be reproduced, stored in a retrieval
system, or transmitted in any form or by any means, electronic, mechanical,
photocopying, recording, or otherwise, without the prior written permission
of the copyright holder.

Printed in the United States of America

1 2 3 4 5 6 7 8 9 10 09 08 07 06

Contents

Cover: Mike Newell (right) directs Daniel Radcliffe in
Harry Potter and the Goblet of Fire.

CHAPTER 1

How Movies Get Made

Director Steven Spielberg was ten years old when he made his first movie. He borrowed a small movie camera from his dad. He used no actors — just his electric trains and other toys. First he filmed a toy train speeding from right to left. Next he filmed a toy train speeding from left to right. Then he cut back and forth quickly, so the trains seemed to be hurtling toward each other. His finished film took three minutes. He called it *The Last Train Wreck*.

Making a short home video is still a great idea for a young filmmaker. But that's not what Steven Spielberg does today. When he made *War of the Worlds* in 2005, hundreds of people worked on his film. Well-paid actors played the major roles. A small army of carpenters and painters built the sets. Highly skilled people did costumes and makeup. Computer wizards added the special effects.

CELEBRITY SNAPSHOT
Steven Spielberg

Born: December 18, 1946, in Cincinnati, Ohio

Film Career: Director, producer, screenwriter

Academy Awards: Winner for directing *Schindler's List* (1993) and *Saving Private Ryan* (1998)

Other Top Films: *Jaws; Close Encounters of the Third Kind; Raiders of the Lost Ark; E.T. the Extra-Terrestrial; Jurassic Park; Amistad; War of the Worlds*

Backstory: When Spielberg was growing up in the 1950s, he loved science-fiction movies. The young director made his first full-length film in 1964. Called *Firelight*, it had a sci-fi theme. Today, his movies *Close Encounters of the Third Kind* and *E.T.* are considered sci-fi classics. Spielberg returned to science fiction in 2005 with *War of the Worlds*. The movie is a remake of a 1950s hit.

Steven Spielberg (left) gives directions to Dakota Fanning (center) and Tom Cruise (right) on the set of *War of the Worlds*.

Team Efforts

Nearly all movies shown in theaters are team efforts. They use many people with many different skills. Three key jobs on the team are directing, screenwriting, and producing. Sometimes one person does all three jobs. More often, one person directs the film, and others do the writing and producing.

Directors control the creative part of making movies. They choose the actors. Then they coach the actors on how to play their parts. They work with the set designers, costume makers, and camera operators. When filming ends, the work of editing

This complex shot from *War of the Worlds* required the skills of many different people.

the film begins. Top directors with the right to "final cut" get to control how the finished film will look.

Every movie has a script. The script includes the words the actors say. (Sometimes actors add their own lines.) The script also tells where and when each scene takes place. The script is often called a screenplay. The person who writes the screenplay is known as a screenwriter.

Producing the Film

Producers handle the business part of making movies. They raise the millions of dollars that a movie may cost to make. Often this money comes from a film studio. The major U.S. film studios all have offices in Hollywood in southern California.

Film studios are in business to make movies — and to make money. When a studio puts up millions of dollars to make a film, it expects to have some control over the finished work. For example, a studio may tell a director it will greenlight a project only if a famous movie star is in it.

Every film has a budget. The budget shows how much money the director can spend. Producers make sure everyone gets

Behind the Scenes:
Making a Hollywood Movie —From Start to Finish

PRE-PRODUCTION
- "The pitch" — offer idea to studio
- Make budget (based on how much money studio says it will provide)
- Decide where and when film will be shot
- Write and revise script
- Hire actors
- Design sets and costumes

PRODUCTION
- Make daily shooting schedule
- Build sets as needed
- Set up lighting
- Choose cameras and lenses
- Film scenes with actors in full costume and makeup

POST-PRODUCTION
- Make rough edit of movie
- Add special effects
- Re-record sound as needed
- Add music
- Create movie posters, trailers, and Web site
- Make final cut
- Distribute film to theaters

paid. They also make sure everyone is on time. Most films are shot in a few weeks or months. Costs go up quickly when a movie falls behind schedule.

Indie Films

Some directors are not happy with the studio system. They don't want to change their movies just because a studio wants them to. They don't want to use famous movie stars if they think lesser-known actors will do a better job. They don't want to make movies that look like everyone else's. They want to film their own stories in their own way.

Directors can avoid the studios by making independent (or "indie") films. When the film is finished, the director may show it at an indie film festival. Studios then bid for the chance to market the movie.

Some indie films have very low budgets. What is the cheapest full-length film ever made? It might be *Tarnation*. Shown in theaters in 2003, this indie movie was made for only $218!

Keisha Castle-Hughes (left) starred in *Whale Rider*, a popular indie film directed by Niki Caro.

CHAPTER 2

Types of Films

Sixty or seventy years ago, people expected to see several kinds of movies at the same show. A short cartoon — maybe with Mickey Mouse or Bugs Bunny — came first. Next came a newsreel, with news from around the world. Finally, the feature film was shown. The feature was a full-length movie, usually at least ninety minutes long. Sometimes theaters had a double feature — two full-length films for the price of one ticket.

Today, feature films run about two hours long and sometimes much longer. For example, *Lord of the Rings: The Return of the King* is more than three hours long. The short films shown before the feature are almost always ads. Some of these ads are for other movies. These ads are known as movie trailers. Trailers are also called previews or coming attractions. A very short preview is known as a teaser trailer.

Comedy, Drama, and Everything in Between

Feature films inspire different kinds of feelings. Some make you laugh. Others make you cry. Movies can make your heart thump and your palms sweat. They can teach you things you never knew — or help you see the world in a whole new way.

Films come in various genres (JOHN-rz). *Genre* is a French word that means "type" or "kind." Each genre has its own rules. Films may combine genres in fresh and interesting ways.

Behind the Scenes:
Awards for Directing and Writing

Dozens of film groups and film festivals hand out prizes each year. The film industry votes on Academy Awards for directing and screenwriting as well as for best film. These awards are often called Oscars.

Directors belong to the Directors Guild of America. This group began giving out directing awards in 1948. The awards cover films, TV shows, and ads.

Screenwriters are members of the Writers Guild of America. Each year, it honors outstanding movie, television, and radio scripts.

Comedy is a popular genre. Gross-out comedies like the *American Pie* films use crude, sexual jokes and bathroom humor to make you laugh. Romantic comedies focus on characters who fall in love with each other. Drew Barrymore often

Behind the Scenes:
Documentary Films

A documentary is based on real life. Instead of actors and sets, it uses real people and real places. Like other kinds of movies, a documentary should tell an interesting story. But this story must be true to the facts.

Documentaries have been made about many different subjects. For example, *Spellbound* is a true-life film about a spelling bee. This film came out in 2002. Another first-rate film is *March of the Penguins*. It shows how male and female penguins survive the bitter winter cold.

appears in romantic comedies. Her films include *50 First Dates* and *Fever Pitch*. Adam Sandler, Julia Roberts, and Jennifer Aniston also often act in romantic comedies.

Many people enjoy action-adventure films. Some of the most successful films in this genre have comic-book heroes. Recent films based on comic books are *Batman Begins* and *Superman Returns*. *Spider-Man* and *Spider-Man 2* combine action scenes with a love story.

The documentary film *March of the Penguins* was a surprise hit in 2005.

A drama is a film that deals with a serious subject. *Rocky* and *Cinderella Man* are boxing dramas that have happy endings. *Million Dollar Baby* is a drama about a female boxer. Its ending is very sad. *Lost in Translation*, with Bill Murray, has moments that are funny and sad at the same time.

Tastes, Trends, and Series
You probably have friends who love one kind of film and hate another. For example, some people really enjoy horror movies. Other people can't stand them.

Fashions in film genres can change. For example, Westerns used to be very popular. Many decades ago, stories about "cowboys and Indians" were sure to attract big audiences. But as attitudes toward Native Americans changed, old-style Westerns seemed outdated. On the other hand, science-fiction films are much more popular than they used to be. The turning point was 1977, when *Star Wars* became a huge hit.

Some film series have lasted a long time. Studios figure that if you liked the first *James Bond* spy film, you'll like the second . . . or the twentieth. The *Star Trek* series spanned ten feature films and hundreds of TV shows. The *Harry Potter* films have been huge hits. Hollywood hopes fans of the boy wizard will want to see the remaining films in the series.

CELEBRITY SNAPSHOT
Sofia Coppola

Born: May 14, 1971, in New York City

Film Career: Director, producer, screenwriter, actress

Academy Awards: Winner for writing *Lost in Translation* (2003)

Other Top Films: *The Virgin Suicides*; *Marie Antoinette*

Backstory: Sofia Coppola is the daughter of director Francis Ford Coppola. She has been involved with movies her whole life. Bill Murray describes her way of working with actors as quiet but tough. "Sofia is made of steel," he says. "She's very polite about it. She nods her head and says, 'You're right, you're right. But this is what I want to do.' And it works."

Sofia Coppola and actor Bill Murray worked together on *Lost in Translation*, which was filmed in Japan.

What the Screenwriter Does

Every good movie needs a good script. If the movie is a comedy, the script needs to be funny. If the movie is a drama, the story needs to be believable. If the movie is an adventure story, the script needs to be exciting, so viewers won't get bored.

Writing for the screen is not the same as writing for the printed page. When you write books or stories, you can tell the reader all about your characters. You can say where they go, what they see, and what they do. You can even describe how they think and feel. Every word you write becomes part of the story.

Writing a Scene

A screenplay tells a story mostly through dialogue. Dialogue is what the characters say to each other. For example, in a short story, you might write,

"Emma and Hannah greeted each other like long-lost friends." In a screenplay, the dialogue might go:

"Hannah: Emma!

"Emma: Hey, where have you been? You've cut your hair!"

Screenplays are written as a series of scenes. Each scene begins with a brief note, called a slug line. This note tells whether the scene takes place indoors or outdoors. (In screenplays, an indoor scene is marked as "Interior" or "INT.") The slug line also tells where the scene happens and at what time of day. A slug line for the scene with Hannah and Emma might read:

"INT. MATH CLASS. DAY."

A scene may also include notes for the actors and director. For example, suppose a girl named Mia is jealous of Hannah and Emma. She doesn't want them to be friends. Just after Hannah and Emma greet each other, you might write:

"CUT TO: Mia frowning."

This line tells the director to follow the shot of Hannah and Emma with a shot of Mia. It also tells the girl playing Mia the emotion she needs to show. Mia doesn't have to speak. The wordless shot will show viewers that she feels left out.

Behind the Scenes:
From the Book to the Script to the Screen

The *Harry Potter* movies are based on the novels by J. K. Rowling. Steve Kloves adapted one of the novels for his screenplay for *Harry Potter and the Goblet of Fire*.

From the J. K. Rowling novel, page 411:
There was just no getting around the fact that [Ron's] robes looked more like a dress than anything else. In a desperate attempt to make them look more manly, he used a Severing Charm on the ruff and cuffs. It worked fairly well; at least he was now lace-free, although he hadn't done a very neat job, and the edges still looked depressingly frayed as the boys set off downstairs.

From the Steve Kloves screenplay:
Ron: What are those??
Harry: My dress robes.
Ron: Well they're alright. No lace, no dodgy little collar.
Harry: Well I expect yours are more traditional.
Ron: Traditional?? They're ancient!
I look like my great aunt Tessie. . . .
I smell like my great aunt Tessie. Murder me, Harry.

In a funny scene from *Harry Potter and the Goblet of Fire*, Harry and Ron get ready for the Yule Ball. Notice the ruffles on Ron's outfit!

Adapted and Original Screenplays

Many scripts are based on works that first appeared somewhere else. These works can be novels, short stories, articles, or other movies. A script based on another work is called an adapted screenplay. For example, the three *Lord of the Rings* films are based on the classic book series by J. R. R. Tolkien. Peter Jackson, who directed the films, also helped write the scripts. His wife, Fran Walsh, worked with him.

If the idea for a film is entirely new, the script is called an original screenplay. One of today's best screenwriters is Charlie Kaufman. He wrote the script for *Eternal Sunshine of the Spotless Mind*. This quirky film stars Jim Carrey and Kate Winslet. In the movie, they fall in love and then break up. Carrey goes to a doctor who has a machine that erases the bad memories — and many good ones, too. The movie asks, If you spend your life trying to avoid getting hurt, what else are you giving up?

Jim Carrey prepares to lose his memory in *Eternal Sunshine of the Spotless Mind*, written by Charlie Kaufman.

CELEBRITY SNAPSHOT
Peter Jackson

Born: October 31, 1961, in New Zealand

Film Career: Director, producer, screenwriter

Academy Awards: Winner for writing and directing *The Lord of the Rings: The Return of the King* (2003)

Other Top Films: The first two parts of the *Lord of the Rings* series, *The Fellowship of the Ring* and *The Two Towers*; *King Kong*

Backstory: Jackson shot all three *Lord of the Rings* films in New Zealand in eighteen months. *The Return of the King* won a total of eleven Oscars.

Peter Jackson (left) discusses a scene with Ian McKellen, who played Gandalf in *The Lord of the Rings* films.

What the Director Does

A script consists of words on a page.
A movie consists of sights and sounds.
Turning words on a page into scenes
on a screen is the job of the director.
Will a scene be fast or slow? Light or
dark? Loud or quiet? Happy or sad? The
director has to answer questions like these
— and many more.

Pre-production

The time before shooting begins is called pre-
production. During this period, the director
may ask the writer to make changes in the script.
Rewriting is a normal part of making a movie.
Most directors help choose the actors. Directors also
work with the actors to make sure they understand
their roles as shown in the script. Director Mike
Leigh works the opposite way. He starts with an
idea for a plot but no set script. Before the cameras
roll, he works with the cast for months. Everything
in his movies grows from the way the actors relate
to each other.

At the other extreme, many directors use pre-production time to plan their movies shot by shot. They lay out the film in a series of rough sketches. These sketches are called storyboards. The storyboards serve as a road map for making the movie.

Director Tim Burton likes to sketch everything. His sketches tell the set and costume designers what he wants. He also shares his drawings with the actors. When Johnny Depp starred in *Edward Scissorhands*, he found the drawings very helpful. "I'd read the script," he recalls. "But Tim's drawings said everything. . . . They haunted me."

Burton's sketches helped Johnny Depp understand his character in *Edward Scissorhands*.

CELEBRITY SNAPSHOT

Tim Burton

Born: August 25, 1958, in Burbank, California

Film Career: Director, producer

Top Films: *Beetlejuice; Batman; Edward Scissorhands; Charlie and the Chocolate Factory*

Backstory: Tim Burton takes a small sketchbook and a set of watercolor paints almost everywhere he goes. "I think best when I'm drawing," he told a *New York Times* newspaper reporter.

Burton was an artist before he became a movie director. In the ninth grade, he won an anti-littering poster contest. His poster was displayed on Burbank, California, garbage trucks.

Tim Burton's movies look like nobody else's. Here, the director considers a scene in *Charlie and the Chocolate Factory*.

Production

During the actual filming, everything runs on a tight schedule. This period is when the director is under the most pressure. The sets and costumes must be just right. Every scene must be properly lit. The actors must know their lines. Scene after scene, the director must keep the whole cast and crew on their toes.

Each day, the director goes over the "dailies." Dailies — also called rushes — are films or videos of scenes that have already been shot. Based on the dailies, the director may decide to reshoot one or more scenes. The studio also may want to see the dailies. The dailies show the studio what the director is doing.

Behind the Scenes:

So You Want to Be a Movie Director . . .?

It's easy for a young filmmaker to get started. Discount stores sell simple video cameras for under one hundred dollars. If you can't afford your own camera, you may be able to borrow one from a parent or friend.

Start by writing your own script. Use a room at home as a set. Shoot outdoor scenes in your backyard or neighborhood. Check to see whether your school offers a course in making videos. Many schools have video equipment. Programs on home and school computers make video editing a snap.

About six hundred U.S. colleges and universities have film studies programs. New York University and the University of Southern California have famous film schools.

Some directors shoot each scene from many different angles. They may shoot as much as an hour of film for each minute they use. Other directors hate to waste film. They try to take only the shots they know they'll keep.

Post-Production

The director's work doesn't end when the filming stops. After shooting, the director must shape the film into its final form. This job is called editing or cutting. In the past, pieces of film were actually cut apart, then put back together in a different order. Today, the editing is usually done on a computer.

In post-production, scenes may be moved around. Visual effects, sound effects, and music are added. Sometimes the studio holds test screenings. At a test screening, the director pays careful attention to how the audience responds. If the film is a comedy, the test audience should laugh at the right places. If the jokes don't work, the director may need to recut some scenes.

Top directors like Steven Spielberg and Peter Jackson get the final say on the shape of their movies. They have the right of "final cut." A studio can't make changes without their permission.

Money and the Movies

Movies are an art form. They are also a business. More than 360,000 Americans make their living in the movie industry. Some earn money by making and showing movies. Others work in stores that sell or rent videos.

Each year, Americans spend about $9.5 billion on movie tickets. The average price of a ticket is about six dollars. At the movie, you may also buy popcorn, candy, or soda. Theaters actually make more profit on popcorn than on the movies they show!

Counting the Costs

These days, a typical studio movie costs almost $100 million. Many movies cost much more. For example, the budget for *Spider-Man 3* may go as high as $250 million. *Superman Returns* and *King Kong* had production costs of up to $210 million. *Spider-Man 2* cost about $200 million.

CELEBRITY SNAPSHOT
John Singleton

Born: January 6, 1968, in Los Angeles

Film Career: Director, screenwriter, producer

Academy Awards: Nominated for writing and directing *Boyz N the Hood* (1991)

Top Films: *2 Fast 2 Furious*; *Four Brothers*

Backstory: Singleton is the youngest person ever nominated for an Oscar as best director. He was only twenty-three years old when *Boyz N the Hood* came out. Critics said harsh things about *2 Fast 2 Furious*. But the movie was a big hit in 2003, earning $240 million. Singleton used the profits from that film to help fund his other movies.

John Singleton (left) lines up a shot on *2 Fast 2 Furious*.

The success of *2 Fast 2 Furious* in summer 2003 gave a big boost to Singleton's Hollywood career. Its hot cars, high-speed chase senes, and illegal street racing thrilled many viewers.

Where does all that money go? Everyone who works on a movie gets paid. Famous actors can demand $20 million for one film. Directors and producers may also get a big slice of the profit. A single special effect can cost tens of thousands of dollars.

For every three dollars spent on a film, two go to making the movie. The third dollar is spent on marketing the movie. TV ads, print ads, movie trailers, Web sites all cost money — lots of it.

Behind the Scenes:

The Crawl

At the end of every feature film is a list of people who worked on the movie. This list is called the crawl. For a big-budget film, the crawl may include hundreds of names. Many of the job titles are familiar. Others may be new to you. Here are a few unusual jobs listed in the crawl:

- Gaffer: The head electrician. The gaffer supervises the electrical crew. The gaffer also is in charge of lighting the set.

- Best boy: The gaffer's main assistant. The best boy is sometimes called the second electrician.

- Key grip: The person in charge of moving cameras and related equipment.

- Set dresser: Someone who makes sure that all the items needed for a scene are where they should be.

Measuring Success

Studios measure success in dollars. The first test comes at the box office — how many people will pay to see a certain movie? In 2005, for example, *Star Wars: Episode III — Revenge of the Sith* earned $380 million in U.S. theaters. The film also earned vast sums overseas. Video rentals and DVD sales will further boost profits. So will sales of *Star Wars* toys and video games.

Successes don't come any bigger than *Titanic*. James Cameron's 1997 movie about a doomed ship cost $220 million to make and market. It earned more than $600 million at the box office in the United States alone. Worldwide, the movie made at least $3 billion. That's more than some countries spend in a year!

No wonder some people see the movie business as a way to get rich. And it is — for a few. But most people in the movie industry aren't wealthy. They make movies because that's what they love to do. "I'm not making films because I want to be in the movie business," says director Woody Allen. "I'm making them because I want to say something."

Titanic, **directed by James Cameron, is one of the top movie moneymakers of all time.**

Glossary

Academy Award — also called an Oscar; an award given out by the movie industry.

backstory — the background story to something seen on screen.

dialogue — in a screenplay, the words the characters say to each other.

documentary — a film based on real life that uses real people and real places.

final cut — the finished, edited version of a film.

greenlight — to approve.

market — to sell

nominated — named or suggested as a candidate for a particular honor or position.

post-production — the period after a film is shot, when the movie is put into final form.

pre-production — the period before the movie is shot.

production — the period when the movie is actually filmed.

screenwriter — the person who writes the movie's screenplay, or script.

sets — scenery built for use in a movie or play.

storyboards — sketches that set out a shot-by-shot plan for making a movie.

trailer — an ad for a film; also called a preview or coming attraction.

To Find Out More

Books

Attack of the Killer Video Book: Tips and Tricks for Young Directors. Mark Shulman and Hazlitt Krog (Annick Press)

Steven Spielberg: Crazy for Movies. Susan Goldman Rubin (Harry N. Abrams)

Ten American Movie Directors: The Men Behind the Camera. Collective Biographies (series). Anne E. Hill (Enslow)

Videos

E.T. The Extra-Terrestrial (Universal) PG

March of the Penguins (Warner Home Video) G

Spider-Man 2 (Sony) PG-13

Titanic (Paramount) PG-13

Web Sites

The Internet Movie Database
www.imdb.com
Facts about movies and the people who make them

Cinema: How Are Hollywood Films Made?
www.learner.org/exhibits/cinema
Follow specific links for information about screenwriting, directing, and producing

Publisher's note to educators and parents: Our editors have carefully reviewed these Web sites to ensure that they are suitable for children. Many Web sites change frequently, however, and we cannot guarantee that a site's future contents will continue to meet our high standards of quality and educational value. Be advised that children should be closely supervised whenever they access the Internet.

Index

About the Author

Geoffrey M. Horn has been a fan of music, movies, and sports for as long as he can remember. He has written more than three dozen books for young people and adults, along with hundreds of articles for encyclopedias and other works. He lives in southwestern Virginia, in the foothills of the Blue Ridge Mountains, with his wife, their collie, and four cats. He dedicates this book to the memory of Ann and Man Posnack.